WHAT THE NATIVE AMERICANS WORE

Colleen Madonna Flood Williams

MASON CREST
PHILADELPHIA

NATIVE AMERICAN LIFE

WHAT THE NATIVE AMERICANS WORE

Colleen Madonna Flood Williams

SENIOR CONSULTING EDITOR DR. TROY JOHNSON
PROFESSOR OF HISTORY AND AMERICAN INDIAN STUDIES
CALIFORNIA STATE UNIVERSITY

MASON CREST
PHILADELPHIA

As always, to Paul R. Williams and Dillon J. Meehan with all my love, and for my mother, mother-in-law, grandmothers Alice and Marg, my friend, Carol Hess, and my Aunt Sister Madonna.

Mason Crest
450 Parkway Drive, Suite D
Broomall, PA 19008
www.masoncrest.com

© 2014 by Mason Crest, an imprint of National Highlights, Inc.

Printed and bound in the United States of America.

CPSIA Compliance Information: Batch #NAR2013. For further information, contact Mason Crest at 1-866-MCP-Book

First printing
1 3 5 7 9 8 6 4 2

Library of Congress Cataloging-in-Publication Data

Williams, Colleen Madonna Flood.
  What the native Americans wore / Colleen Madonna Flood Williams.
      pages cm. — (Native American life)
  Includes bibliographical references and index.
  ISBN 978-1-4222-2978-1 (hc)
  ISBN 978-1-4222-8865-8 (ebook)
  1. Indians of North America—Clothing—Juvenile literature. I. Title.
  E98.C8W56 2013
  391.0089'97—dc23
                                    2013007313

Native American Life series ISBN: 978-1-4222-2963-7

TABLE OF CONTENTS

INTRODUCTION

For hundreds of years the dominant image of the Native American has been that of a stoic warrior, often wearing a full-length eagle feather headdress, riding a horse in pursuit of the buffalo, or perhaps surrounding some unfortunate wagon train filled with innocent west-bound American settlers. Unfortunately there has been little written or made available to the general public to dispel this erroneous generalization. This misrepresentation has resulted in an image of native people that has been translated into books, movies, and television programs that have done little to look deeply into the native worldview, cosmology, and daily life. Not until the 1990 movie *Dances with Wolves* were native people portrayed as having a human persona. For the first time, native people could express humor, sorrow, love, hate, peace, and warfare. For the first time native people could express themselves in words other than "ugh" or "Yes, Kemo Sabe." This series has been written to provide a more accurate and encompassing journey into the world of the Native Americans.

When studying the native world of the Americas, it is extremely important to understand that there are few "universals" that apply across tribal boundaries. With over 500 nations and 300 language groups the worlds of the Native Americans were diverse. The traditions of one group may or may not have been shared by neighboring groups. Sports, games, dance, subsistence patterns, clothing, and religion differed—greatly in some instances. And although nearly all native groups observed festivals and ceremonies necessary to insure the renewal of their worlds, these too varied greatly.

Of equal importance to the breaking down of old myopic and stereotypic images is that the authors in this series credit Native

Americans with a sense of agency. Contrary to the views held by the Europeans who came to North and South America and established the United States, Canada, Mexico, and other nations, some Native American tribes had sophisticated political and governing structures—that of the member nations of the Iroquois League, for example. Europeans at first denied that native people had religions but rather "worshiped the devil," and demanded that Native Americans abandon their religions for the Christian worldview. The readers of this series will learn that native people had well-established religions, led by both men and women, long before the European invasion began in the 16th and 17th centuries.

Gender roles also come under scrutiny in this series. European settlers in the northeastern area of the present-day United States found it appalling that native women were "treated as drudges" and forced to do the men's work in the agricultural fields. They failed to understand, as the reader will see, that among this group the women owned the fields and scheduled the harvests. Europeans also failed to understand that Iroquois men were diplomats and controlled over one million square miles of fur-trapping area. While Iroquois men sat at the governing council, Iroquois clan matrons caucused with tribal members and told the men how to vote.

These are small examples of the material contained in this important series. The reader is encouraged to use the extended bibliographies provided with each book to expand his or her area of specific interest.

Dr. Troy Johnson
Professor of History and American Indian Studies
California State University

1 Functional Fashion

Traditional pre-Columbian Native American clothing styles differed greatly from one region to the next. The Tohono O'odham, or Papago, of the Sonoran desert wore clothing made of cotton and leather. Their shoes were typically sandals. Far to the north, the Inuit people of the Arctic used the guts, skins, or furs of musk oxen, polar bears, caribou, seals, snowshoe hares, wolverines, tundra squirrels, and wolves to make clothing. They wore sealskin or caribou boots. The Caribs and Taino of the Caribbean wore little or no clothing and often went barefoot.

All of these **aboriginal** Americans had a few things in common, however. They knew how to dress effectively to survive in their native environments. Using skill and ingenuity, they learned to make clothing using only the natural resources available to them. Clothing was often a reflection, not

A man dressed in colorful traditional dress dances in a powwow in Arizona. The colors, patterns, and styles of Native American regalia are often meaningful, giving clues to the wearer's tribe and his or her status within the tribe.

This Native American warrior of the Piegan tribe was photographed wearing traditional attire. Warriors often used different parts of "power" animals, such as feathers, fur, and antlers, to make themselves look more fierce.

only of lifestyle and climate, but also of personal status, class level, or rank within the family and society. Thus, Native American clothing was made to be both functional and fashionable.

Every attempt has been made by the author to be respectful and accurate. The past tense is used not to suggest that Native American culture is a thing of the past. It is used solely to signify that these descriptions are referring to Native American cultures from the pre-European contact to early-European contact periods. To learn more about Native American clothing, the author recommends that you study the clothing of individual tribes, bands, and groups of Native Americans at your local library or on the Internet. The Further Reading section at the end of this book has a good list of books and Web sites to start with. §

This painting, by American artist George Catlin, depicts one method Native Americans of the Great Plains used to hunt buffalo during the 19th century. Hiding under animal skins to camouflage their bodies and their scent, hunters were able to get close enough to a herd to get a good shot.

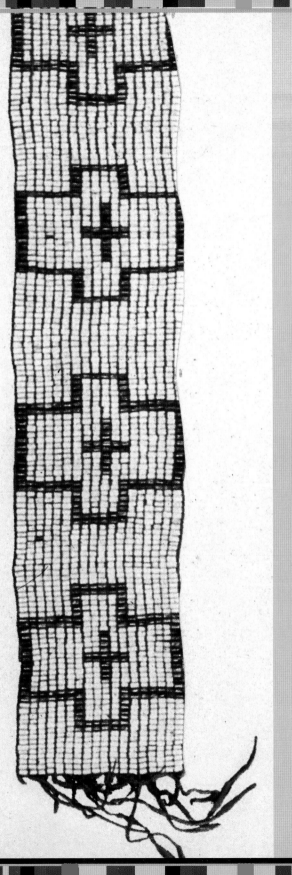

This belt was made around the year 1785 from wampum, tiny beads used as currency by many Native American tribes. The white beads were generally rated at only half the value of the purple beads made from the quahog, or hard clam. Wampum belts were often worn to demonstrate wealth.

2 Gustowehs, Roaches, and Wampum Belts

In the regions surrounding the Great Lakes and woodlands of the Northeast, clothing had to be adjusted accordingly for the different weather conditions of the four seasons. Clothing that was warm in the winter but cool in the summer was created from leather made from deer and other animals. This clothing was decorated with porcupine quills, moose-hair embroidery, and floral designs made from **wampum**. Wampum belts, moccasins, and headbands were worn. Brass, copper, and feathers were used for ornamentation as well.

Beads were made from bone, wood, freshwater clamshells, animal teeth, and stones. Hair combs were carved from bone. The Great Lakes groups perfected a style of weaving that utilized **rush** and **hemp**. Using this process, they wove strips that could be used for necklaces, belts, and headbands.

The Iroquois dressed mainly in deerskin clothing, as they frequently hunted whitetail deer. In the Ohio Valley, the people hunted buffalo. Thus, buffalo hides were commonly used by these people for shirts, dresses, robes, and footwear. As the Micmac, Abenaki, and Mahican often hunted moose, their clothing was commonly fashioned from moose hides.

Haudenosaunee women of this region stitched two deerskins together at the shoulders to make dresses. They then wrapped belts around their waists to hold the dresses in place. By wrapping and securing a tanned deerskin about the waist, women also made deerskin skirts.

A finger-woven cloth was made from the fiber of the nettle plant. Finger weaving was a type of braiding, tying, or knotting of fiber used to produce cloth. Women wove these nettle shirts and wore them beneath their dresses. Belts and sashes were also made from nettle or hemp. The Tuscarora wore shirts woven from hemp. Their name for themselves, Ska-Ru-Ren, means "shirt-wearing people."

Deerskin leggings were also worn. These covered and protected a woman's legs from her knees to her ankles. The leggings were secured to a belt that held them up. Moccasins were worn on the feet.

A Haudenosaunee man's **breechcloth**, leggings, and moccasins were typically made from tanned deerskin. All of these items were often decorated with quillwork or beadwork. Woodland men also wore sashes, belts, and turbans woven from nettle or hemp.

A man from the Secotan or Powhatan tribes of Virginia would wear a breechcloth, also. From the back of his breechcloth, he might

This picture provides a closer look at the beadwork, fringe, and adornments of a buckskin dress made in the traditional Otoe-Missouri style.

> **Porcupine- or bird-quill embroidery is a unique North American art form. Women of the Northeastern woodlands used vegetable dyes to color the quills. Sinew thread, made from animal tendons and ligaments, was used to secure the quills to clothing, medicine bags, shoes, and other items. Intricate floral designs were embroidered using porcupine quills.**

have an animal tail hanging down. Fringed skin bags were a sign of rank and were often hung from the sides of men's breechcloths in this region of North America.

Children wore clothing much like that of their parents. Small infants were often simply wrapped in soft furs. Iroquois and Delaware men, women, and children wore slippers made from twined cornhusks in the summer.

People also wore deer, bear, and other fur or hide wraps during the colder parts of the year. These were usually just untailored, tanned hides draped over the shoulders and around the body. Mineral and vegetable dyes were used to paint plant, animal, spirit, and clan symbols on these robes. Moose-hair tufting and quillwork were also used to adorn these robes.

The Haudenosaunee wore a type of feathered headwear, called a **kastoweh** or gustoweh (pronounced gah-sto-wha). This hat was fashioned out of three pieces of black ash. One piece wrapped around the head, crossing the forehead and both ears. The other two pieces were fitted, one from front to back, and the other from side to side, over the head. These pieces were then sewn to the piece that wrapped around the head.

The Iroquois nations each had their own particular version of this common style of headdress. The number and position of the feathers were different for each Iroquois nation. The deer antlers attached to their gustowehs identified the council members of all the six nations. If a council member was removed from office, it was called a de-horning because he was stripped of his ceremonial deer antlers. The clan **matron** from that person's clan selected his replacement.

The Cayuga gustoweh featured a single feather pointing to one side. The Seneca wore one upright feather in their gustowehs. The Oneida headgear had two vertical feathers. The Mohawk gustoweh had three upright feathers. One feather was worn upright, while another pointed to the right on an Onondaga gustoweh. The Tuscarora headpiece was topped with many feathers.

Another common piece of headgear was the roach. Men wore roaches for special ceremonies and also in battle. A roach was a crown of animal hair. This animal hair would cover the man's head and drape over his shoulders. The short hair from deer tails or moose hair and long porcupine guard hairs were often combined to make roaches.

A roach spreader was used to keep the roach in place on a man's head. This was a comb made out of bone, horn, or antler. A braid from the man's head was pulled through a hole in the middle of the roach. The spreader had one hole in it through

17

NATIVE AMERICAN LIFE

which this braided piece of hair could be pulled. The braid was then pushed through a second hole in the roach spreader and fastened with a small wooden peg. This held the roach in place atop the man's head.

Clan necklaces were one commonly worn piece of jewelry. These featured the beaded, moose-tufted, or quilled designs of clan crests. Earrings were fashioned from bone, antler, shells, and other natural resources. In many tribes, both men and women wore earrings. The Algonquian tribes of Virginia wore pearl jewelry.

Grizzly-bear claw necklaces were highly regarded. A warrior could obtain such a trophy in a number of ways. Either the warrior killed a number of grizzly bears and collected their claws, or he inherited the necklace from an older relative. If the warrior killed an enemy man who was wearing such a treasure, then he would generally strip the body of its bear-claw necklace and keep it as his own.

Wampum bracelets and belts were worn also. These were made from freshwater clamshells and were traditionally purple and white. The background of the design would be purple, and the design itself was worked in white. These were worn for more than decorative purposes. Most wampum belts and bracelets were documents that recorded important events. Those who had knowledge of their significance could read the symbols and designs fashioned into these items.

Masks were worn for special ceremonies and rituals. The Iroquois had a special group of healers called the False Face

Society. The members wore masks carved from live basswood trees. These masks took the form of faces seen in the carvers' dreams. Iroquois men and boys also made and wore cornhusk masks during the midwinter ceremonial rites.

Huron warriors were well known for their skillfully made body armor. They made and wore armor that consisted of shields, breastplates, and loincloths made from wooden slats.

When the Europeans began making contact with the Native Americans of this region,

Body adornment was popular throughout the Northern United States. Popular tattoos were clan emblems, geometric shapes, and personal spirit guides. These crests and symbols might be painted on as well. Animal grease was used to make hair shine. Wampum, feather, and quillwork items were worn as hair ornaments. A person who had tattoos, body paintings, and hair ornaments was considered well groomed.

many things changed. Women began using glass beads obtained from the Europeans to decorate clothing, belts, footwear, and other items, and different types of cloth found their way into Native American villages.

At first, few Native Americans had enough access to cloth to use it for clothing. Headbands, turbans, and sashes were fashioned from this rare European material. In most cases, however, only the most important tribe or clan members owned such cloth items.

As contact with the Europeans increased, more and more aboriginal Americans were able to obtain cloth and incorporate it into their wardrobes. Native American seamstresses began to fashion clothing that looked more and more like that of the Europeans. This clothing was still usually decorated with traditional tribal designs and clan crests, however. **S**

This Iroquois mask was used for the ceremonies of the False Face Society. The members of this society carved their masks from a living tree. In spring and fall they went from house to house in their village, shaking turtle-shell rattles and chanting to drive away the demons that caused illness and disease.

21

NATIVE AMERICAN LIFE

This Cherokee "booger" mask was worn to represent the spirit of a white man threatening their culture. Men of the tribe wore these masks to ward off evil spirits and influences.

3 Turkey Cloaks and Palm Fiber Breechcloths

In the Caribbean heat, most Taino men went without clothing. Others wore a cotton or palm fiber breechcloth, called a **nagua**. In a number of Taino villages, the length of this breechcloth was an outward symbol of the man's status in society.

Taino children and unmarried women did not wear clothing. A married woman wore a cotton or palm fiber cloth that covered her from waist to mid-thigh, serving as a clear outward symbol of her status as a married woman.

Body painting was done by both sexes for special occasions and religious ceremonies. Many Taino wore earrings, nose rings, and other jewelry made from gold, pearls, seashells, and stones.

A Timucua woman of Florida wore fringed skirts or dresses made of Spanish moss. The men wore cloths wrapped between their legs and then tied tightly around their waists. One end of the cloth was used to secure it about the waist, and the other was pulled between the legs and then up and through the waist belt created by the rest of the cloth. Timucua children wore little or no clothing in warm weather. In cold weather, the Timucua were known to wear cloaks made of bird feathers for warmth.

The Timucua men wore breastplates made from **conch** shells. They also sometimes had conch shells hanging down from their waistbands. Bracelets were worn around the knees and consisted of one or two conch shells connected by sinew or string made from plant fibers.

All of the Timucua people wore bone earrings. Men and women also decorated themselves by wearing tattoos. By cutting a design into the skin and then rubbing ash into the cuts, a Timucua could create permanent tattoos. After the ash was rubbed into the wound, vegetable and mineral dyes were poured over it, adding color to the tattoo.

The Florida Calusa men wore only tanned deerskin breechcloths. These breechcloths were held up by belts indicative of one's position in the tribe. Calusa women wore skirts and dresses made from woven Spanish moss and palmetto leaves.

Cherokee men wore breechcloths, leggings, shirts, and moccasins. Buckskin capes were worn about the shoulders in colder weather. Men wore cloaks made from turkey and eagle feathers for important occasions and spiritual rituals.

Cherokee women wore dresses, **yokes**, cloaks, and moccasins of buckskin. Porcupine quillwork, copper and shell jewelry, as well as clay and stone decorations were widely used by Cherokee women. One design in particular was referred to as a "Strength of Life" design. This was a whirlwind that symbolized the movement of the Cherokee people around their ceremonial fires. Cherokee decorative clothing designs often featured four logs, the sun, a whirlwind, and a weeping eye.

The clothing worn by Choctaw women prior to contact with the Europeans consisted of a blouse and short skirt made from animal hide. Sometimes, women wore mid-calf–length buckskin dresses. The bottoms, arms, and yokes of these dresses were decorated with fringe. When footwear was necessary, women wore moccasins with leggings or a sort of high-top moccasin that extended up past the calf. Most Choctaw women simply went barefoot.

Choctaw men wore breechcloths and moccasins. When traveling, they wore long pants made of animal skins. A tunic, or pullover shirt, with long sleeves was often worn when traveling. These shirts were also worn during periods of cold weather.

In the winter, the Choctaw wore outer garments of animal hide and furs. They tucked their leggings into their moccasins to keep their legs warm and dry. The Choctaw wore moccasins when traveling, but often went barefoot at home.

Both men and women wore their hair long. Sometimes it was worn braided; other times, it was left to hang loosely about the head and shoulders. Special hairstyles were worn for certain occasions and religious ceremonies.

Choctaw clothing was often decorated with designs featuring combinations of lines and geometric shapes, such as diamonds, circles, and crosses. The circle and cross are believed to symbolize the sun and the stars. The diamond-shaped trim found on some Choctaw items is believed to symbolize and show consideration

25

NATIVE AMERICAN LIFE

and appreciation for nature.

During the years that the European missionaries were making their first contacts with southeastern Native American groups, Chickasaw women still tanned buffalo hides for robes. They tanned other skins and furs as well and used them to make clothing for themselves and their families.

Chickasaw women made dresses out of two deerskins and personalized them with shells, quillwork, and beadwork. They also made deerskin leggings, shirts, and loincloths—all decorated with beads and small shells. The Chickasaw men, women, and children all wore moccasins onto which the women put beautiful multicolored designs. The beads were made from wood, shell, or bone. Moccasin designs were usually made so that the person wearing the shoe saw the design as being right side up instead of upside down. This way the shoes were more pleasing to wear.

Chickasaw men painted their faces. On their heads, the men wore

A Seminole chief named Grizzly Bear wears ornate western clothes and carries a gun in this drawing from the early 19th century. European colonists began to influence the lifestyles of some tribes during the 18th century. Native Americans traded with settlers for clothing made from cotton fabric, which was more comfortable than the animal hides and furs the native tribes had used until that time.

27

NATIVE AMERICAN LIFE

Prior to European contact, the Cherokee made wooden or **gourd** masks for ceremonial and ritual purposes. These masks often represented evil spirits. After their contact with Europeans and African slaves, the Cherokee adopted an African name for some of these masks.

The term "booger masks" was derived from the African term "bogeyman." Booger masks often represented the evil spirits of white men who were trying to take Native American lands. Today the word "bogeyman" signifies a terrifying (but often imaginary) person or thing.

tin headbands. The men also wore necklaces featuring several rows of curved pieces of tin. Female ornaments consisted of strings of beads worn around the neck; bracelets of silver, tin, or copper on the arms; and metallic rings in the ears.

Prior to European contact, Seminole clothing was similar to that of other southeastern tribes; however, it changed dramatically after contact with the Europeans. When colored European cotton cloths became easily obtained at trading posts, Seminole women began creating colorful patchwork clothing.

Seminole women had sewing machines in their camps as early as 1892. Around this time, Seminole clothing began to feature patterns of different-colored horizontal stripes. The Seminole seamstresses also favored calico fabrics.

The women wore full, floor-length skirts, gathered at the waist and usually with a ruffle about the knee area. A long-sleeved blouse with a cape attached to it was also worn. The blouse was cut short so that the stomach, or midriff, was exposed.

The Seminole men wore long multicolored cotton shirts. Turbans made from plaid wool were colorful additions to their apparel. A belt worn around the waist of the cotton shirt completed his outfit. In cold weather, a colorful coat decorated with ruffles was worn.

Seminole women have been making their distinctive patchwork clothing for over a century now. The art form has been passed down from mother to daughter, in keeping with Seminole tradition. In fact, many Seminole people still wear variations of this type of clothing today.

Prior to contact with the Europeans, Choctaw women often wore a blouse and skirt made of cotton trade cloth. In the winter, they wore woolen shawls. White aprons with colored trim and ruffles became commonplace amongst Choctaw women. §

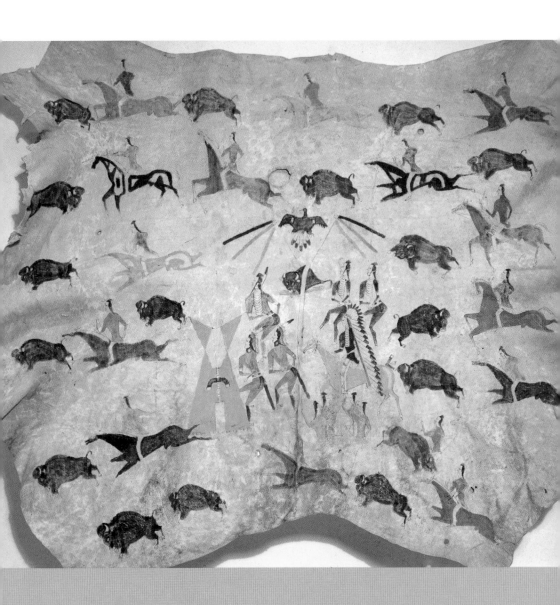

This buffalo robe was decorated with the story of a great hunt. The hides of the bison were as important as the meat to the Native American tribes of the Plains. Robes, leggings, and even tepees could be made from tough buffalo skin.

Buffalo Robes, Elk-Tooth Dresses, and Twine Sandals

The clothing styles found on the Plains were often similar in basic structure, but the symbols, designs, and some of the materials used to create these adornments differed from group to group. The buffalo hide was the most commonly used material. Not only was clothing made from buffalo hides, but so too were shoes, accessories, tools, utensils, ceremonial items, children's toys, and homes. The buffalo played a major role in the life of almost every Native American living in the West.

Elk teeth were the most prized of all dress decorations. They were placed in rows that went from the shoulders and neckline of the dress all the way to the bottom hem—provided a woman had enough of the valuable teeth. If only a few teeth were owned, then the rows of teeth were spaced farther apart. Sometimes, a dress featured just a single row of teeth that had been added to the bottom or top of a row of beadwork.

Plains men wore shirts, breechcloths, and full-length leggings. They often had beautifully decorated war shirts. Women wore dresses and shorter leggings. Moccasins were the customary footwear of the Plains. **Ponchos** added a layer of protection from the weather.

The most common Plains dress was a basic slip dress. This was a large piece of hide that was pulled over the wearer's shoulders. The sleeves were separate pieces that were fastened about the neck and under the arms. Sinew, thread, plant fiber twine, or leather strips were used to lace together the two sides of the dress that hung over each shoulder.

The two-hide dress had sleeves sewn into it. The hind legs of an animal's skin were often used to create these sleeves. An opening was cut for the neck, and the sleeves were sewn, laced, tied, or sometimes cut in such a manner that they were left to fall openly about the arms. Vegetable and mineral dyes were used to paint tribal colors and symbols onto these dresses.

Many items of clothing worn by people of the western tribes featured fringes. They were sewn around the bottom edges of shirts and dresses. Sometimes, a separate piece of material with fringes cut into it was added across the chest and back of a dress or shirt. Fringes were not just a fashion statement. They also served a useful purpose. Fringes on a garment would help to repel rain, keeping both garment and wearer from getting too wet.

The clothing that Native Americans wore every day was usually not as ornate as regalia, or ceremonial clothing. Often, daily wear merely featured a narrow band of beading or fringe. Ceremonial and special clothing was elaborately decorated, however. Armbands and anklets were often part of a man or woman's dance outfit. These were highly decorated with beadwork or made from strips of fur.

A Native American dons traditional feathered dress for a powwow in California. Because eagles are a protected species in North America, anyone who wishes to use their feathers in regalia must place a special order and receive government approval. A request for eagle feathers can take up to two years to fill.

Buffalo robes were used to keep people warm and to keep track of tribal history. The tribal artists of the Plains, known as "winter count keepers," marked the passing of years in winters by painting pictographs onto buffalo robes. The important events in the lives of their people—natural disasters, wars, hunts, births, and deaths—were all recorded on these types of wearable documents. Painted in a traditional pattern and with traditional symbols, a buffalo robe provided an easily interpreted history of years gone by. A winter count keeper could share the events recorded on a buffalo robe and, in doing so, help keep great leaders and events of the past alive in the memories of his people. Winter count keepers were respected and admired for their skill at reading buffalo robes and for their diligent attention to the recording of important events for record keepers and tribal members of future generations.

Other common articles of clothing in this region included belts, ornamental headgear, and necklaces. Spiritual items, herbs, sewing articles, totems, or **awl** and knife cases were worn hanging from belts. Eagle feathers were highly prized as decorations for headgear.

The clothing worn by men and women of Plains tribes changed greatly after the Europeans began trading cloth to them. Wool or cotton trade cloth replaced the buckskin and buffalo hide apparel worn throughout the Plains region. Warriors, traders, and scouts obtained pieces of European clothing and wore them. When United States troops began to travel throughout the West, soldiers' clothing began to turn up in Native American villages. Native American women began to sew clothing mimicking the styles they saw worn by European men and women.

Skin dresses, shirts, and pants were still used for ceremonies or gatherings. War shirts, headdresses, and moccasins continued to be made in a traditional manner. However, the beads and items used to decorate these pieces of daily wear and regalia changed. Glass beads obtained from Europeans began to be used by many of those natives who could acquire such decorative materials.

In the Great Basin area, people often went without clothing during the warmer seasons of the year. A married woman might wear a skirt woven from natural fibers found in the area. Sometimes, Great Basin women fashioned these small skirts from sagebrush bark. Their husbands and the other adult men in the region merely wore belts or loincloths.

The men would hang medicine bags, tools, and knives from their belts. The women would hang these items from the waistbands of their skirts. Men and women wore earrings and occasionally decorative ties in their hair. Women in this region also wove hats. For the most part, the children in this region went without clothing.

Footwear consisted of basic animal-hide moccasins for the winter. In the summer, many individuals in the Great Basin region wore woven **tule** and cattail sandals. Children would most often be barefoot.

Rabbit skin capes were worn in the winter for warmth. These capes were woven from rabbit skins so that they were made of fur on both the outer and inner sides. Not only did they serve as winter garments, they also were used as blankets and beds during the cooler seasons.

35

NATIVE AMERICAN LIFE

Susi Yazi, a Navajo woman, wears turquoise jewelry and a traditional blanket near the mesas in Monument Valley. The Navajo people are known for their blankets, which are carefully woven in beautiful, intricate patterns. The precious stone turquoise was valued for protection against bad fortune. It is still admired for its beauty and durability.

The women used looms to make these woven rabbit skin capes. First, the rabbit skins had to be prepared. The women would clean and tan them. Next, the skins had to be cut into long, inch-wide strips. After the rabbit skins were cut into strips, they were fashioned into an almost yarn-like material that could be worked on a loom. The women wove these pieces into knee-length capes that were worn tied about one's neck.

The Seri of Mexico wore garments made of pelican skins and woven plant material. Seri women wore jewelry fashioned from pieces of seashells, seeds, and reptile or other animal vertebrae. The Seri also often tattooed or painted their faces and other body parts.

After contact with the European culture, the Seri, like other tribes, began to wear colorful cotton clothing. Seri women wore long, brightly colored trade cloth dresses draped like **saris** around their bodies. The Seri tradition of face tattooing began to diminish after contact with Europeans also.

The Hopi and Zuñi were masters at weaving a native Southwestern cotton plant into cloth. This cotton provided them with the fiber needed to create their intricate weavings. Using plant and mineral dyes, they created different-colored cloths and wove them into bright geometric patterns. Colored patterns also adorned the clothing of most of the Pueblo peoples.

The Navajo wore moccasins that had a hard sole made of hide. The hard soles protected their feet from cactus needles and other sharp desert objects. As the Navajo were often on the move, sturdy footwear

37

NATIVE AMERICAN LIFE

George Catlin was an artist who traveled around the North American continent painting portraits of Native Americans and writing descriptions of their clothing, housing, and lifestyles during the mid-1830s. Here is his description of an Osage warrior:

An Osage warrior, from a southern latitude, entirely primitive in his habits and dress; his head shaved, and ornamented with the graceful crest manufactured from the hair of the deer's tail and horsehair (a uniform custom of the tribe), his robe of the buffalo's hide, with the battles of his life emblazoned on it; his necklace made of the claws of the grizzly bear; his bow and quiver slung upon his back; and his leggings fringed with scalp-locks taken as trophies from the heads of enemies slain by him in battle.

Many Native Americans today take offense at the term "primitive." When one studies their culture, it becomes quite apparent that their habits and dress were far from primitive.

was an important piece of clothing for them. The Navajo were also known for their woven blankets.

For the Mayan men of southeastern Chiapas in Mexico, the wardrobe consisted of short pants worn with a knee-length shirt. The men also wore hats, twine sandals, and red sashes. Their shirts were, and still are, called *huipils*.

The huipil is a rectangular-shaped shirt. It features a complex **brocaded** and woven intersecting T-shape that covers the arms, front, and back of the shirt. Brocaded weaves are still done today on an age-old style of hand loom by women, and sometimes men, in the Chiapas Maya villages.

The symbolic decoration of a huipil represents elements of the world, sky, and spirits. The patterns and meanings brocaded and woven into the huipil have survived since the classic Maya period. Travelers can see these patterns carved into the walls of the palaces and buildings of the ancient Mayan settlements.

The traditional wardrobe of a Mayan woman from Chiapas would include a long wraparound skirt of wool, a sash, and a cotton blouse or tunic. Women also wore a rebozo, or shawl; they did not wear shoes. ⑤

A Crow warrior would have worn this eagle headdress during battle. The idea for the headdress probably came to the warrior during a vision, and was the brave's personal war symbol. Other birds and animals could also be used for this type of headdress, depending on which creature had acted as a messenger during the vision. However, the eagle was believed to provide particularly great power to the wearer.

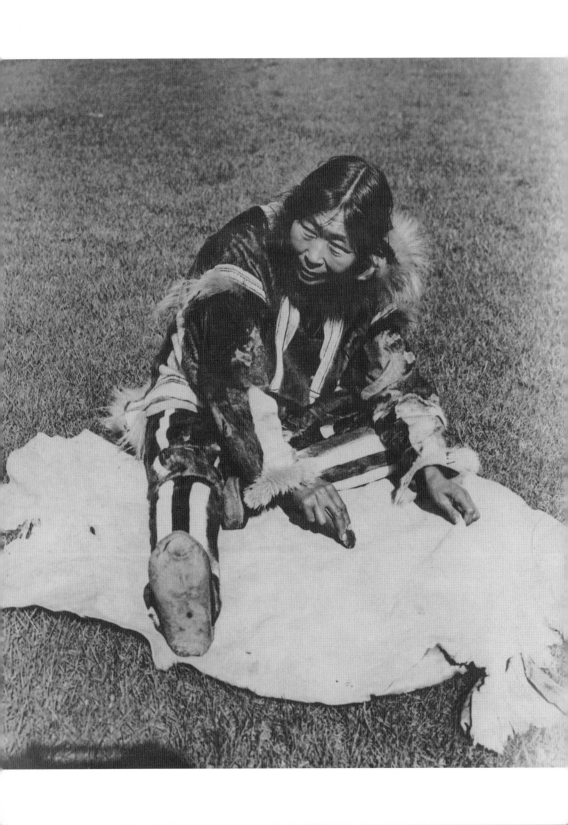

5 Willow Headbands, Cedar Bark Capes, and Gut Parkas

To stay warm, both men and women in the northwestern region wore woven rabbit, squirrel, fox, or groundhog fur robes. The Interior Salish made blankets woven from the wool of mountain goats. Men wore buckskin shirts, breechcloths, leggings, and moccasins. Women wore buckskin leggings beneath two-piece buckskin dresses. Again, there was a great variety of decorative styles and raw materials used for clothing in this area.

An Inuit woman from Alaska prepares an animal skin so that it can become a garment. Hides had to be cleaned and dressed before they would make a proper coat or leggings. Some tribes removed the fur completely and tanned the hide, turning it into soft but tough leather.

The Pacific Northwest is a North American rainforest region. Consequently, its native peoples learned to make hats, shoes, and clothing out of spruce roots and cedar bark to keep the rain off their heads, feet, and bodies. The Eyak, Tlingit, Haida, and Tsimshian tailored animal furs, mountain goat wool, tanned skins, and cedar bark into clothing. These materials helped to keep them warm and dry.

Special clothes were worn during certain festivals or ceremonies. Regalia, or ceremonial clothing, found in various areas of the region might consist of Chilkat robes, Raven's Tail robes, painted leather clothing, intricately decorated tunics, beaded or embroidered leggings, elaborately decorated cedar bark moccasins, ground squirrel robes, and masks.

Chilkat robes were named for the Chilkat people. The earliest-known Chilkat robes were made from animal skins and featured painted designs. Later, Chilkat robes were woven from mountain goat wool and cedar bark. A Raven's Tail robe was also made using mountain goat wool. These robes were made using a weaving process referred to as two-strand twining.

A Chilkat robe is rectangular in shape and features a long V-shaped bottom hem decorated with fringe. Both sides of the robe are decorated with fringes also. Chilkat robes were usually white, yellow, red, black, blue, and green.

After contact with Europeans, the style of robes changed in this region. Blankets obtained through trading were used to make clothing and robes more and more often. Glass beads were also obtained from the Europeans—first Russian fur traders and later English and Spanish traders. The beads were used for decorative purposes, replacing more traditional decorative items such as shells and bone.

Northwest coastal tribes made and wore masks that told entire legends. These masks had several movable parts on them and more than one face. The first face of a mask was usually that of an animal or spirit.

The second face was generally a human image. These animal/human face masks symbolized the Northwest belief that human spirits could come in the form of animals and that animal spirits could come in the form of humans. The masks also united the animal and human worlds into one. Such masks were an important part of Inuit and Yu'pik life.

The clothing of the Inuit people had to do two main things: keep them warm and keep them dry. Parkas, or *kuspuks*, were worn as outer garments. Tops were worn beneath these outer garments. Outer and inner pants, socks, and boots were also worn. These layers were important in the struggle to stay warm and dry. Inuit shirts and pants were often made from caribou skin. The fur of an outer garment faced outward. The fur of an inner garment was sewn to face the wearer's body.

Women's parkas featured hoods that were large enough to carry a baby. Men's hoods were much smaller. Fur ruffs were sewn onto the sleeves, hoods, and bottoms of men's, women's, and children's parkas. The fur ruff of a parka hood was designed to protect the wearer's face from the cold, wet arctic winds.

Gloves and socks were made from available skins and furs. The fur was usually turned toward the wearer's skin on these garments. Gloves were tied together with a leather strip. Then, this strip was placed around the neck, which prevented the individual from losing the gloves if they had to be removed for some reason.

The Inuit made waterproof outer garments from the intestines of seals, walrus, and other sea creatures. These were highly effective

43

NATIVE AMERICAN LIFE

at keeping the wearer dry. Often, they were worn by Inuit seal and whale hunters. Gut parkas were sometimes decorated with fur, ivory, tufting, or shell beadwork.

The Aleut lived in a wet climate, so they, too, needed waterproof clothing. They also used animal-gut parkas to protect themselves from the cold and wet maritime climate in which they lived. Aleut clothing was often decorated with puffin feathers and beaks; ivory, bone, and wooden ornaments; and beautiful animal furs.

The Aleut carved wooden masks for ceremonial use. They also wore special clothing that was often specific to a particular dance or ritual. Aleuts wore wooden hats that were made by steaming wood until it could be bent into the proper shape. The hats were then decorated with seal or sea lion whiskers and painted with colorful dyes made from vegetables or minerals.

Men of the Nootka tribe would usually wear only a few pieces of jewelry. Their women wore cedar bark skirts. For protection against

A native woman living in the Nunavut province of Canada stays warm in a thick parka, which is made primarily from animal skin and fur. The people of the Far North have retained their culture and clothing more successfully than other native tribes, because it is still necessary to live off the land in Alaska and the Subarctic.

the cold during the spring, summer, and fall months, the Nootka people wore cedar bark robes and cone-shaped cedar bark hats. In the winter, some of the Nootka people wore sea otter skins and bearskins. These Nootka were the families of the best hunters or the richest members of society. The Nootka who dressed in raccoon or squirrel were generally the poorer members of their society.

This clan hat was worn by a Tlingit chief. It was made to represent a bear, one of the most powerful and fearsome animals in North America. Animal symbolism was meant to give the wearer the strength and dominance of the animal.

Yup'ik clothing was made from a wide variety of natural materials. Bird skins, fish skins, marine mammal hides, and other animal hides were used over the years to create Yup'ik apparel. Clothing had to be warm and waterproof—particularly for the Yup'ik hunter.

Outer garments for hunters and fishermen were often made from fish skins or from the intestines of marine mammals. Yu'pik women created waterproof coats, pants, and boots with these natural resources. Spotted seal and other available pelts were used to decorate the clothing.

Boots were insulated by sticking grass into them. Grass was also sometimes used as a waterproof thread. Yu'pik women made baskets

47

Men from the Ojibwa tribe perform a Snow Shoe Dance to
thank the Great Spirit for the first snowfall. The ingenious
invention of snowshoes made walking in snow easier. The wide
shoes distributed the wearer's weight across a larger space,
making it less likely that he or she would sink through the snow.

out of grass. These baskets were woven so tightly they could hold water or other fluids.

Yu'pik women made gloves and mittens from spotted sealskins. Fur was used as a decorative border, but also as an insulating material and shield against the wind for parkas. Boots were often made of salmon skins. Caribou skins were used to make inner pants and shirts.

The Athabascans' regalia varied from group to group. Leaders often wore **dentalium** shell necklaces as part of their regalia. Men wore beaded coats and tunics. Women also wore beaded tunics. Beaded dance boots were sometimes part of a woman's regalia.

Traditional daily wear for an Athabascan was made of caribou or moose hide. Moose- and caribou-hide moccasins and boots were decorated to match the wearer's parka, if possible. Different styles of moccasins were made to suit varied purposes and weather conditions.

49

Whaling crews brought many Europeans to the Northwest coastal areas and to the coastal areas of the Far North. These men brought cloth, glass beads, and other items to the Native Americans that they encountered. After trading began, wool and cotton materials were available to the native people. As a result, parkas and inner clothing began to reflect the influences of European styles. Russian influences also changed the dress in these parts of the Americas. §

NATIVE AMERICAN LIFE

 **Cotton Armslings and Head Cloths**

In the high plateau area of Mexico, men of the Aztec tribe wore loincloths. Aztec women wore loose tunics and skirts. All of these clothing items were made from cotton. Long cloaks or capes were worn by high-ranking Aztec officials and nobles as symbols of their elevated status in society.

Aztec clothing was decorated with exotic feathers, furs, shells, metals, and pieces of gold. Cotton clothing was dyed and painted with vegetable and mineral dyes. Any member of Aztec society who could afford it wore gold jewelry.

The most beautiful apparel was reserved for Aztec royalty. The ruling class would dress in elaborate headgear and elegantly decorated robes. The larger a person's headpiece, the more important he or she was in Aztec society. The finest weavings were reserved for members of the upper class as well.

Although many tribes made their clothes from animal hides, others stitched and wove their own textiles from plants. This Magazua woman in Mexico is creating an intricate pattern from colorful threads, which are used to make dresses, shirts, bags, and belts.

In pre-Columbian times, it was common for an elite Inca society member to have a death mask made for his or her mummy. This death mask would be made of gold and finely decorated. The mummies of lower-class Incas often had death masks as well. However, their death masks were made of clay or wood and were decorated with less finery than those of their noble counterparts. A metallic, disk-shaped mask that featured movable ears was discovered in the Moon Pyramid, located in Moche, Peru.

The clothing of the Maya of Guatemala was divided into two categories. The upper-class Maya wore cotton. The peasants wore clothing made from tree bark. This material is called tapa. Lower-class Mayans of Guatemala would go barefoot or wear sandals made of twine.

The cotton fabrics reserved for the upper class were beautifully decorated with brilliantly colored feathers. These feathers were sometimes woven right into the cotton fabrics. The upper-class Maya of Guatemala wore leather belts and sandals, also elaborately decorated.

In South America, the Araweté of Para, Brazil, are a culture of hunters and gatherers. The men have long, thick goatees and usually go around without any clothing. The Araweté women wear four tube-like pieces of clothing made from weaving a native cotton. This cotton is dyed with **urucum**. Their four pieces of clothing consist of a waistband, a skirt, a blouse that is much like an armsling, and a headcloth. The people of this region have dressed like this for many years and have not changed their style of dress much since contact with the Europeans. Even today they have minimal contact with outsiders.

Almost all of the members of their culture wear earrings made from **arara** feathers, arranged to look like flowers. The men's earrings are shorter than the women's.

For women, external pieces of clothing are often inherited. However, one piece of clothing—an inner waistband worn by all women after puberty—is never inherited. Clothing for the women is woven using traditional looms, made of two **babassu**-leaf spindles stuck into the ground. Hammocks are also made using these looms.

This fez-style hat came from the Inca culture in Chile, around 1570. Decorated elaborately with feathers and a colorful design, this hat would have been saved for special occasions and festivals.

53

Natives in Peru wear colorful replicas of Inca costumes during a parade.

Girls begin wearing their outer skirts early in childhood. At the age of seven, they begin to wear their armsling-like blouses. These blouses are made for carrying babies. The inner waistband is worn from the time the girl reaches puberty until her death.

The Inca of the Andes favored a style of clothing that featured dazzling colors and feather decorations. Some of the finest robes and cloaks of the Inca were made with feathers woven directly into cotton cloths. Wool from the Incas' llama herds was also used for clothing, as were chinchilla pelts.

The basic components of Incan clothing were the loincloth for both sexes, short tunics for men, and long dresses for women. These garments were topped off with a poncho. For footwear, sandals were worn or the Inca went barefoot. An outfit might be made complete with a woolen cap or turban, if the weather warranted such headwear.

Tie-dying is an art practiced in the Andes and dates back to pre-Columbian times. When cloth is tie-dyed, parts of it are wrapped or knotted to keep the dye off those areas. The technique is used to create beautiful multicolored cloth for garments.

Today, many **indigenous** women of the Andes still wear a rectangular piece of fabric, called a manta, as a shawl. Across their backs and shoulders and on top of their mantas, they tie slings that are used to carry whatever items they need to take from place to place with them. The colors, patterns, and figures found in the manta can be used to identify the area of the Andes where it was woven.

In the valley of Otavalo in Ecuador, the men attire themselves in white pants and white shirts. On their heads, for protection from the sun, they wear hats. For warmth, they wear wool ponchos. Their sandals are made of a canvas-like material.

The women of this valley wear white blouses, the borders of which are decorated with floral designs. Necklaces made from ceramic beads or coral are worn to dress up the blouses. These women also wear wraparound skirts. Their sandals are made of a canvas-like material, like the men's sandals. Woolen cloths are used to carry things by wrapping them into the cloth and then slinging it across the woman's back. §

55

NATIVE AMERICAN LIFE

CHRONOLOGY

Before 10,000 B.C. Paleo-Indians migrate from parts of Asia and begin settling throughout the Americas.

10,000–5000 B.C. Medicine-wheel spiritual sites are built in the Great Basin region.

6000–5000 B.C. The subarctic regions are settled as the climate begins to warm with the waning of the last Ice Age.

5000–3000 B.C. Earliest-known organized Native American settlements are built in the Southeast.

1400 B.C.–A.D. 1500 Northeastern woodland cultures rise and prosper.

A.D. 300–900 Maya civilization reaches its zenith.

300 Native Americans begin settling in the Plains region and migrating with the buffalo herds and according to the seasons of the year.

700–1300 The Anasazi and Hohokam prosper in the Southwest.

1200–1700 The Pacific Northwest tribes begin settling, hunting, trading, and thriving along the Northwest coast.

1492–1502 Columbus explores the West Indies and Central America.

1521 The Spanish destroy Tenochtitlán, the Aztec capital..

1630–1770 The Spanish build ranches in Mexico and introduce horses to North America.

1830 Congress passes the Indian Removal Act.

1838 Cherokee are forced to move from the Southeast to Oklahoma on the "Trail of Tears."

1876 George A. Custer and his troops are defeated at the Battle of the Little Bighorn by Sioux.

1886 On September 3, Geronimo surrenders at Skeleton Canyon in Arizona.

1890 Massacre at Wounded Knee Creek, South Dakota.

1924 Congress declares all Native Americans to be United States citizens, entitled to the right to vote.

1968 American Indian Movement (AIM) begins to grow and become a political force for the empowerment of Native Americans.

2010 November marks the twentieth anniversary of the celebration of National American Indian Heritage Month.

2013 Recent government estimates indicate that more than 5.2 million Native Americans live in the United States and Canada.

NATIVE AMERICAN LIFE

GLOSSARY

aboriginal the earliest-known people to inhabit a region.

arara a type of parrot.

awl a pointed tool used for marking surfaces or piercing small holes (as in leather or wood).

babassu a palm tree that grows in tropical northeastern Brazil.

breechcloth a cloth worn about the loins or hip area; also known as a loincloth.

brocade to create raised designs on a piece of fabric.

conch any of various large, spiral-shelled marine gastropod mollusks.

dentalium burrowing marine mollusks with a tapering tubular shell; also known as tooth shell.

gourd any of various hard-rinded inedible fruits often used for ornament or for vessels and utensils.

hemp a tall plant belonging to the mulberry family, the fiber of which is often used for making cord and rope.

indigenous having originated in or occurred naturally in a particular region or environment.

kastoweh traditional headgear of the tribes of the Iroquois nations, also called a gustoweh.

matron a married woman usually marked by dignified maturity or social distinction.

nagua a cotton or palm fiber breechcloth.

poncho a blanket with a slit in the middle so that it can be slipped over the head and worn as a sleeveless garment.

rush a marsh plant with cylindrical, hollow stems often used for plaiting and weaving.

sari a garment consisting of several yards of lightweight cloth draped so that one end forms a skirt and the other a head or shoulder covering.

tule a plant belonging to the bulrush family.

urucum a small tree that produces beautiful pinkish-white flowers and later bright red fruit clusters; the small red seeds, when crushed, produce a powder used by Brazilian natives to decorate their bodies and utensils.

wampum small beads made from shells, sometimes threaded on string, often made into belts, and used as historical documents, for decoration, for ceremonial purposes, or for trading purposes.

yoke a fitted portion of a garment, usually around the neck, shoulders, chest, or waist.

FURTHER READING

Barnes, Ian. *Historical Atlas of Native Americans*. London: Cartographica Press, 2009.

Brasser, Theodore. *Native American Clothing: An Illustrated History*. Buffalo, N.Y.: Firefly Books, 2009.

Hoffman, Elizabeth DeLaney. *American Indians and Popular Culture*. 2 vols. Santa Barbara, Calif.: ABC-CLIO, 2012.

Johansen, Bruce E. *Encyclopedia of the American Indian Movement*. Greenwood Press, 2013.

Johnson, Michael, and Richard Hook. *Encyclopedia of Native Tribes of North America*. Buffalo, N.Y.: Firefly Books, 2007.

Oberg, Michael Leroy. *Native America: A History*. Malden, U.K.: Blackwell Publishing, 2010.

60

INTERNET RESOURCES

http://www.csulb.edu/colleges/cla/departments/americanindianstudies/faculty/trj
Website of the American Indian Studies program at California State University, Long Beach, which is chaired by Professor Troy Johnson. The site presents unique artwork, photographs, video, and sound recordings that accurately reflect the rich history and culture of Native Americans.

http://www.snowwowl.com/peopleinuit1.html
This Web site offers information on the history of various Native American cultures of the Arctic Circle region.

http://www.kstrom.net/isk/mainmenu.html
This web site contains extensive resource material on Native Americans.

http://www.nativeweb.org/resources
This web site features a collection of resources and links to informative Native American Web sites.

http://nmai.si.edu/home
This site contains fascinating information collected by the Smithsonian Institution about Native American history and culture.

INDEX

NATIVE AMERICAN LIFE

PICTURE CREDITS

CONTRIBUTORS

Dr. Troy Johnson is chairman of the American Indian Studies program at California State University, Long Beach, California. He is an internationally published author and is the author, co-author, or editor of twenty books, including *Wisdom Spirits: American Indian Prophets, Revitalization Movements, and Cultural Survival* (University of Nebraska Press, 2012); *The Indians of Eastern Texas and The Fredonia Revolution of 1828* (Edwin Mellen Press, 2011); and *The American Indian Red Power Movement: Alcatraz to Wounded Knee* (University of Nebraska Press, 2008). He has published numerous scholarly articles, has spoken at conferences across the United States, and is a member of the editorial board of the journals *American Indian Culture and Research and The History Teacher.* Dr. Johnson has served as president of the Society of History Education since 2001. He has won awards for his permanent exhibit at Alcatraz Island; he also was named Most Valuable Professor of the Year by California State University, Long Beach, in 1997 and again in 2006. He served as associate director and historical consultant on the award-winning PBS documentary film *Alcatraz Is Not an Island* (1999). Dr. Johnson lives in Long Beach, California.

Colleen Madonna Flood Williams is the wife of Paul R. Williams, mother of Dillon Joseph Meehan, and daughter of Patrick and Kathleen Flood. She lives in Alaska with her husband, son, and their dog, Kosmos Kramer. She has a bachelor's degree in elementary education with a minor in art.

Uncle Henry & Aunt Henrietta's
H·O·N·E·Y·M·O·O·N

Uncle Henry & Aunt Henrietta's
H·O·N·E·Y·M·O·O·N

by Nicole Rubel

 Dial Books for Young Readers ♦ New York

To my family

Published by Dial Books for Young Readers
A Division of NAL Penguin Inc.
2 Park Avenue ◆ New York, New York 10016
Published simultaneously in Canada by Fitzhenry & Whiteside Limited, Toronto

Copyright © 1986 by Nicole Rubel
All rights reserved
Library of Congress Catalog Card Number: 85-15944
Printed in Hong Kong by South China Printing Co.
First Pied Piper Printing 1988
W
1 3 5 7 9 10 8 6 4 2

A Pied Piper Book is a registered trademark of
Dial Books for Young Readers,
a division of NAL Penguin Inc.,
®TM 1,163,686 and ®TM 1,054,312.

UNCLE HENRY & AUNT HENRIETTA'S HONEYMOON
is published in a hardcover edition by
Dial Books for Young Readers.
ISBN 0-8037-0498-4

The paintings, which consist of black ink and colored markers,
are color-separated and reproduced in full color.

One night Uncle Henry and Aunt Henrietta came to baby-sit my sister Pearl and me. They were our favorite sitters because they always told us such good stories.

As Pearl and I were playing, Uncle Henry suddenly chuckled.
"What's so funny?" we asked.
"That song on the radio is the same one Aunt Henrietta and I danced to on our honeymoon.

"We were crossing the Pacific Ocean on a cruise ship having
a wonderful time.

"The moon was full and the stars were twinkling when the
ship started to sink!"
"Were you scared?" we asked.
"No, I wasn't, but Henrietta held onto me tightly.

"We were in the water for only a minute when a whale passed by
and picked us up!"
"How lucky!" cried Pearl.

"No, no. You're wrong, Henry," said Aunt Henrietta. "It wasn't a whale. It was a canoe paddled by fierce natives.

"They carried us to their village and danced around us while the cook cut up vegetables and threw them into a large kettle.

"I stayed calm but Henry looked nervous until they led us to
the kettle and served us cream of coconut soup."

"No, no, Henrietta," said Uncle Henry. "We ate octopus and sea snails that night. Don't you remember? The next morning we flew off to the Sahara for a trek across the desert.

"We were following an ancient trade route when I discovered that our guides were lost. Henrietta was very thirsty so I . . .

"took the lead and soon we came to an oasis. We drank fresh
water and rested in the shade of some palm trees —"

"No, no! You're wrong, Henry," exclaimed Aunt Henrietta.
"Don't tell me you've forgotten our hike across Antarctica.

"We stopped to rest and I climbed a hill to look around. Suddenly the hill moved! I was carried away on top of a polar bear."

"Weren't you frightened?" we asked.

"Nope," said Aunt Henrietta. "The bear called over some of his friends and we went sledding until Henry arrived —"

"Sledding!" said Uncle Henry. "By then we were almost at the
top of Mount Everest. Everything was going well until . . ."

"Henrietta lost her balance and fell into the basket of a passing balloon."

"Come on, Henry," said Aunt Henrietta. "We never climbed Mount Everest. We left Antarctica and wandered onto a nearby launching pad. A flight was just leaving for the moon, so we volunteered and blasted off. An hour later Henry began to feel dizzy so I —"

"Shhhh! The children are asleep," whispered Uncle Henry.

"Did you have fun last night?" asked Mom and Dad at breakfast.

"Yes," said Pearl. "Uncle Henry and Aunt Henrietta told us about their honeymoon to the Sahara and Antarctica."

"And sinking ships and fierce natives," I said.

"How odd," said Mom, "I'm pretty sure they went to a resort on Lake Miniwanna. Let's get the family album."

Henry learning how to water ski.

Henry and Henrietta after a day at the beach.

Henrietta exercising in the gym.

Henry and Henrietta dining at Chez Rare Rabbit.

"No, no," said Dad. "Mom is confused. Those pictures were taken on their wedding anniversary. They spent their *honeymoon* at Niagara Falls. . . ."

ABOUT THE AUTHOR

"Nicole Rubel has produced another gem of a picture book. . . . Bravo, Bravo, Bravo!" raved *Children's Book Review Service* about *Uncle Henry & Aunt Henrietta's Honeymoon* (Dial). And *Publishers Weekly* applauded *Pirate Jupiter and the Moondogs* (Dial) with: "Rubel has attracted an army of boys and girls who will embrace this blastoff into space." She has also written and illustrated *Bruno Brontosaurus* and the Sam and Violet books, and has illustrated *Woof! Woof!* (Dial) and the Rotten Ralph series.

Nicole Rubel was raised in Coral Gables, Florida, and received a Bachelor of Fine Arts degree from the Boston Museum School in affiliation with Tufts University. She enjoys raising orchids and other exotic plants and is working diligently on perfecting a recipe for muffins. She lives in Miami with her husband.